"The Cow Killers"

WITH THE AFTOSA COMMISSION IN MEXICO

—FOR FLOYD & JUDY
DE SU AMIGO—

Bill
- Leftwich -

"The Cow Killers"

With the Aftosa Commission in Mexico

DRAWINGS BY BILL LEFTWICH
TEXT BY FRED GIPSON

UNIVERSITY OF TEXAS PRESS, AUSTIN
1956

Manufactured in the United States of America

Second Edition
Third Edition
Fourth Edition
Fifth Edition

Library of Congress Catalog Card No. 56-11771

To The People of rural Mexico, patient in the face of men and work they had no way of understanding.

Publisher's Foreword

In March of 1949, young Bill Leftwich, of Crystal City, Texas—former student at Texas A. & M. College, soldier of World War II—went into Mexico to serve as a livestock inspector for the Aftosa Commission in its fight against the foot-and-mouth disease.

Stationed in the vicinity of Zacapú and Pátzcuaro, in south central Michoacán, Leftwich spent some three years rounding up and corralling cattle, chasing pigs, roping and tying down wild mountain steers, inspecting every cloven-footed animal in his district for symptoms of the virus.

When the day's job was done, unlike most of his co-workers, Leftwich did not hurry back into town to spend the remainder of the evening bending an elbow at the cantinas. Instead, he returned to his wife and baby and to bend an elbow over his drawing board.

With a keen sense for the dramatic, an eye for detail, and plenty of natural ability though little training, the young artist set out to record the day's adventures in line and wash. Some of those adventures were sad, some comic, some rowdy, and some tragically bitter. With an uninhibited flare, Leftwich recorded them all.

Along with the drawings, Leftwich kept notes on the events that had inspired them, events full of the flavor of Mexico and having to do, for the most part, with the reaction of the natives to the work of the commission. These stories he related to Fred Gipson, Texas Hill Country author of such books as *Hound-Dog Man, Big Bend, Cowhand, Recollection Creek,* and *Old Yeller.* Gipson converted the stories into the series of vignettes that accompany Leftwich's work in this book. With the exception of Bill Leftwich and Tom Roberts, names of the members of the commission are fictitious.

Austin, Texas
July 15, 1956

Contents

"The Cow Killers"

WITH THE AFTOSA COMMISSION IN MEXICO

CMAPEFA
DIST III
PAN
JUAN BARRIGA T.
JESUS DELPARRAL
CERVEZA
MONTERREY
DELICIOSA
VACINATION
REPORT
B.O.C.R.T
P
Bill

La Comisión

It was called *La Comisión México-Americana para la Erradicación de la Fiebre Aftosa,* and the 1946–47 newspapers told all about it.

The newspapers explained that the organization was a joint commission set up by the governments of Mexico and the United States to combat the dread foot-and-mouth disease that had broken out among the livestock of Mexico. They told of the first discovery of the deadly virus and the alarming rapidity with which the contagion had spread into parts of sixteen states and the Federal District. They pointed out that the health and often the very life of every cloven-footed animal of the Republic was under threat—15 million cattle, 5½ million hogs, 4½ million sheep, and 7 million goats. They predicted that unless control measures were quickly employed the disease was sure to be carried across the country's borders—into Guatemala, with over 3 million head of susceptible livestock, and into the United States, with 173 million head.

Personnel for the commission was made up of scientists, technicians, and field workers of both nations, their numbers at the peak of employment amounting to 1,166 Americans and 7,938 Mexicans. From central offices in Mexico City, these workers were assigned to district offices in various parts of infected and threatened areas. And, since there is no known cure for the disease, preventive measures had to be drastic. Members of the commission were given authority to establish and maintain rigid quarantine lines, inspect and vaccinate all animals in exposed zones, and eradicate all infected ones.

All of this information, plus the vital necessity for speed of action, was made public in newspapers throughout the Republic.

The difficulty lay in the fact that so few owners of Mexico's livestock read the papers.

The People live with their domestic animals as they have lived for generations, in a family-like intimacy often difficult for foreigners to comprehend. They grow them for the same purposes that all men grow livestock—for food, for clothing, for profit. Nevertheless, they still hold for their animals a deep and abiding affection, so that it is nothing unusual for favorite pigs, oxen, or chickens to be housed in the same dwelling that shelters the family.

Also, there was this fact to add strain to the situation: most members of the commission were of another race—arrogant Mexican officials of the ruling *gente decente* class, equally arrogant Texans, New Mexicans, and Arizonans. These were of the white race, a race hated since the coming of the conquistadores, a race that for nearly four centuries has robbed the native, beaten him, starved him, and held him in contempt.

For The People, to have their private lives and the lives of their animals intruded upon by members of this race was a shaming experience. To take orders, often at gun point, from those not of The People, who spoke another language, who violated the customs, who

-Bill-

had little time and less inclination to explain their acts, was a shock and a humiliation. And to stand helplessly by, as they often did, while their beloved animals were herded into pits and shot down in cold blood, filled them with a horror and a tragic bitterness that no amount of explanation could have alleviated.

"What if our animals do have the sickness?" The People charged. "Does an infirmity justify murder?"

So The People resisted; and they were a people with long experience in resisting.

They applied a term of sly derision to members of *La Comisión,* calling them *los matavacas* ("the cow killers"), the implication being that they gloried in killing female cattle for lack of courage to face a bull in the ring.

The People neglected to corral their livestock for inspection. They hid them away in remote and secret canyons. They disclaimed ownership. They had no horses to hire out to members of *La Comisión,* no food to sell, no knowledge of the road leading to the house of a neighbor.

And sometimes, in their fear and ignorance, in their resentment of the power of the Mexican Army and the highhanded ways of the American gringos, they resorted to open and passionate violence.

A Delicate Situation

For the alcalde, or mayor, of a village, the coming of *La Comisión* posed a delicate situation. On the one hand was *La Comisión,* empowered by government authority to demand the corralling and vaccinating of all *ganado.* On the other hand, there were The People, firmly opposed to such outrageous proceedings.

How was one to decide—and still remain mayor? Some, who were astute, avoided making the decision.

La Comisión would arrive in a village. The line-up men would be directed to a house that was like all the other houses. The walls would be of crumbling rock and adobe. The roof would be of sun-baked clay tile. The picket door would sag on its leather hinges, leaving an opening at the lower corner convenient to the free passage of pigs, chickens, goats, and small children.

A gringo would knock at the door. The wife would come out, close the door behind her, and stand waiting, with prepared answers.

"*Señora,* we seek the one in charge of order."
"That is my husband, *señor;* but he is not present."
"Where is he?"
"He is gone."
"Gone where?"
"To the mountains, *señor,*" the wife would say, lifting a hand in a vague, directionless wave toward the range beyond.
"Is there a road into the mountains?"
"Yes. For the burros."
"When will your husband return?"
"Who knows?"
"Tonight?"
"It is possible. But it will be late. Of a certainty, it will be very late, should he return at all."

So there was nothing left for the gringo to do except search out the second man of the village and present to him the printed government form which advised that the mayor must have the cattle corralled and ready for vaccinating three days hence..

Which proved to be a foolish act, of little consequence. For, as was well known in the village, the second man was without learning. And how can a man be expected to follow orders when he cannot read the words?

A Logical Misunderstanding

Working in advance of *La Comisión* were many unscrupulous buyers of livestock. They went among The People and said: "*La Comisión* is coming. The gringos will pick your *ganado* with their needles. The medicine may kill your goats. It may cause your cows to fail in their milk. It may rob your oxen of the strength necessary to draw your plows. It is said that the medicine often causes sterility among your best cows. . . . Consider. Do you not think it wise to sell your *ganado* before *La Comisión* comes?"

The People considered. Were these things true of the medicine? How could they know?

Often The People became confused. Fearing total loss, they were induced to sell their livestock at half its value.

In Celaya, Guanajuato, such buyers convinced The People that the vaccine caused sterility in all creatures.

The day that gringo Dan Real arrived at Celaya with the vacci-

-Bill-

nating brigade, a farmer appeared at the corrals, dragging along a struggling and shrilly protesting woman.

"What passes, friend?" Real inquired.

The farmer said, "This one is my wife. We have fourteen children. I feel that it is now time that she be picked with the needle."

Beware of the Needles!

At Zinapécuaro, in Michoacán, The People were fearful of the great needles that resembled cartridges and were said to be more deadly. They argued long with Dr. Harry Leak, who was in charge of the first work of *La Comisión* in this place.

"We are told that the needles will kill," The People said.

"No, that is not true," Dr. Leak insisted. "The needle does not kill. It is the sickness that kills. The needle is used to prevent the sickness."

But The People were not convinced. Why should they take the word of a stranger and a gringo?

"Allow me to show you," Dr. Leak persuaded. "Allow me to pick one animal that you may see whether the needle kills."

"And if the animal dies?"

"Then *La Comisión* will reimburse you. Here, at the present."

The People huddled together and discussed the matter. At last, one turned to Dr. Leak.

-Bill-

"We will allow you to pick one," he said. "If that one dies, *La Comisión* repays the owner."

The test animal was a white bull. He was a big bull and wild, and he fought hard against having his head drawn up to the post. He continued to fight, even after his head was tied. He was still lunging and bawling and kicking and switching his tail when Dr. Leak drove the needle into his neck.

At that very instant, the bull's legs weakened and crumpled under his weight. He fell and lay lifeless, with only his head held off the ground by the ropes that bound him to the post.

The People cried out in consternation. "See! He is dead! The needle killed him."

"No!" denied Dr. Leak. "He broke his neck. The needle did not kill him. He merely fought the ropes until he broke his own neck."

"But the bull is dead, is he not?" The People demanded angrily. "You picked him with the needle, and now he is dead."

"I picked him, and now he is dead," Dr. Leak agreed. "Nevertheless, the needle did not kill him."

But The People would not believe. The white bull had been alive until picked by the needle and now he was dead. The gringo would pay for the dead bull and he would pick no more *ganado* in Zinapécuaro.

The People were angry, and they spoke with no uncertainty.

So *La Comisión* paid for the white bull, and it was not until later, when he returned with armed soldiers, that Dr. Leak could persuade The People of Zinapécuaro to allow their cattle to be vaccinated.

The Old Woman of Tzengio

"Our cattle shall not be murdered!" agreed The People of the village of Tzengio. They said to one another: "When *los matavacas* come, we will defend our livestock. We will gather in a great mob and fight with knives and pitchforks and scythes and stones. We will not permit *La Comisión* to slaughter our animals."

The People were agreed and very determined.

La Comisión came. The members arrived in an army power wagon. They were eight in number. There was a veterinarian, a captain of the army, a sergeant, a private first class, and four privates.

When members of *La Comisión* encountered the sullen mob awaiting them in the town plaza, they stopped the truck. The captain got out. He lifted a hand in greeting and attempted to explain.

"We have not come to kill your cattle," he assured The People. "We have not even brought our needles to pick them. We come only to inspect, to learn if your livestock has the sickness."

-Bill-

The People were aroused with fear and hatred, but the words of the captain seemed fair. The men considered. Was the captain to be trusted?

The old woman, Teodora Marta, saw their hesitancy and was ashamed. She cried out to the men in a taunting voice: "*Qué pasa, hombres?* Are you men—or he-goats?"

Then she lunged forward and stabbed the captain in the chest with a huge knife.

The first soldier was armed with an automatic rifle. He jammed a cartridge clip into the gun and brought it to his shoulder.

But the mortally wounded captain cried out: "No! Do not shoot! Our orders are not to shoot!"

The soldier hesitated. It was only for a moment, but after that it was too late.

The men of the village were quick to act after the old woman had goaded them and opened the fight. They flung themselves upon the soldiers. They tore the guns from their hands. They stabbed them with knives. They dragged them to the ground and beat their heads with stones. They gouged the eyeballs from the sockets of the dead captain's head and mutilated the bodies of the others.

One soldier escaped. He fought through to a nearby store, where the storekeeper slammed the door shut behind him, saving him from the enraged mob. But he had already received horrible wounds and lived only until the following day.

The People of Tzengio had agreed that their cattle should not be murdered.

As Anyone Can See

On an inspection trip between the towns of Naranja and Tiríndaro, gringo inspector Bill Leftwich and Sergeant Paulino Guillén Álvarez came upon a Tarasco Indian driving six cows. Each cow had a calf at her side.

The inspector stopped the jeep and searched the cattle for the ear tags that would indicate that they had been vaccinated. He saw none and said, "These cattle have not been vaccinated."

Sergeant Álvarez said to the Indian, "Why are these animals not vaccinated?"

The Indian stared at the sergeant while he considered what answer to give. At last he said, "I cannot answer that question, *señor;* for these are not my cattle. They merely go the way I go."

Sergeant Álvarez said, "In that case, will you do me the favor of assisting me in catching these cattle? They must be vaccinated."

The sergeant held out a rope to the Indian, but the man drew back.

-Bill-

"Why," he demanded indignantly, "should I assist you in catching cattle that are not mine? Catch them yourself. I refuse."

Sergeant Álvarez was a genial man who knew and understood The People. Most of the time he exercised great patience. But this day had been a long and difficult one. He had dealt with too many of The People. He was weary of their excuses.

In sudden anger, he struck out, backhanding the Indian with such staggering force that the man's hat flew straight up, to settle back at a comical angle across his ringing head.

When the startled Indian regained his balance, he straightened his hat on his head. He stood and considered the angry soldier. Then he smiled faintly and bowed.

"*Señor,*" he asked politely, "would you do me the kindness to lend me your *reata?* As anyone can see, these cattle must be vaccinated."

A Terror to The People

Ay! There was this lieutenant of the Mexican cavalry. A terror to The People was that one.

One might say in his mind, "I will fight to defend my cattle from the needles of *La Comisión.*" But of what value were mere thoughts when the lieutenant came in advance of *La Comisión?* The will to fight was no remedy.

The lieutenant and his soldiers would arrive in a village without warning. To his soldiers, he would give orders.

"Get this one," he would command, pointing. "Get that one. Get me several of the citizens."

Instantly, the soldiers would seize four or five of The People and drag them to where the lieutenant had other soldiers preparing hang ropes.

Then, without cause, without trial, without explanation, without heed to the lamentations and pleas for mercy, the lieutenant would give orders that these innocent ones be hanged.

Circo

And hanged they were.

Their eyes bulged and their tongues protruded from their mouths, and their bare feet danced in the thin air.

The People looked on in horror.

Just an instant before death would have claimed these innocent ones, they were let to the ground, while five more of The People were seized and made ready to take their places.

At last, some citizen would cry out in desperation: "What passes, my general? What do you wish of us?"

Then the lieutenant would smile and speak in soft words. "Why, only this, *señores: La Comisión* wishes to vaccinate here today. Will you do us the courtesy of corralling and making ready your cattle?"

Many citizens would answer quickly: "But why not, my general? We can be ready immediately. Why did you not explain at the beginning?"

Then the lieutenant would say, "My method saves many words!"

A Spirit of Industry

Such a spirit of industry as did move *La Comisión!* Such an alarming urge to endeavor! Such shocking and unbelievable tricks would its members resort to in their efforts to suck The People into this same bewildering vortex of incredible activity!

The men would come on a village and say: "Corral your pigs. Corral your cattle. Corral your sheep and goats. Have them ready. Thursday, we come to pick them with the needle."

And on Thursday they would come!

They came to the village of Cuanajo in this manner. They saw that the pigs had not yet been corralled according to orders delivered three days ago. They singled out the largest, most productive sow in the village. They roped and dragged the squealing creature into their power wagon. Then they rushed about the village, chasing and roping and vaccinating other pigs.

The owner of the sow became anxious. "Why do you hold my

pig?" he inquired. "Why not pick her with the needle and release her, as you do the others?"

The gringo said: "We keep her. We take her to the soldiers quartered in Pátzcuaro. Soldiers have great and constant hunger for fine fat pigs."

The owner of the sow was stricken with this news. "Is there no remedy?" he pleaded. "Is there nothing to be done?"

The gringo shrugged. "Who knows?" he said. "If you could persuade every man in the village to bring his pigs to this same corral, it is possible that we would refrain from feeding your sow to the soldiers."

How that one did scurry about the village, seeking out every possessor of pigs! How he did plead with them to bring their pigs to the corral in order that his sow might be spared!

Such was his speed of activity and eloquence of tongue that—as astonishing and unbelievable as it may seem—*La Comisión* vaccinated 803 pigs in that corral before the darkness of night shut down!

Of What Value Are Words?

So consuming was the desire of *los matavacas* to pick animals with their needles that they came even on fiesta days.

They arrived at a certain ranch during a fiesta when the celebration had reached that high and glorious peak that speaks of near-empty bottles.

To the owner of the ranch a gringo *matavaca* said: "Why are the pigs not corralled? You were advised."

"*Sí, señor.* But this is fiesta day." And the ranchero held up his bottle to prove it.

The gringo said, "That is no excuse. In Mexico there are too many fiesta days."

"But, *señor!*" the ranchero exclaimed, "that is impossible. On fiesta days, one may cease all labor. He may visit with his friends. He may drink. He may dine. He may dance. He may make love to the beautiful women. One does not work on fiesta days. How, then, can there be too many?"

-Bill-

The gringo said impatiently: "Well, everyone works on *this* fiesta day. You will now proceed to chase pigs!"

"But, *señor,* I have guests. By invitation!"

"Then your guests may assist in chasing pigs!"

Quick anger flushed the face of the host. Of what value are words in the face of such stupid and insulting arrogance?

At that very instant, one of the host's fine sows came to root a muddy and friendly snout against a soldier's leg. The soldier's foot lashed out, brutally kicking the surprised sow's feet from under her. A second soldier fell upon the animal, holding her down while the vaccinator unsheathed his needle.

A great rage seized the host, and the thought came to him: *When words fail, there is always the machete!*

He drew with lightning speed. The heavy, razor-edged blade flashed in the sunlight. It swept down at an angle calculated to sever the vaccinator's head from his shoulders.

It was a mighty blow, but an unfortunate one. A soldier saw it coming and called out a warning. The vaccinator flung himself aside. The blade whistled past his neck with the thickness of a hair to spare. It struck the pig's head, cleaving it open from east to west.

A third soldier fell upon the irate host. He clubbed the man to the ground with the butt plate of his rifle, then struck him more blows. The remainder of the soldiers swung their rifles to their shoulders and brought them to bear upon the guests.

As a result, the guests corralled the pigs, the host lay long unconscious, the slashed sow died, and the fiesta was completely spoiled.

The Nature of a Mule

So heartless, *los matavacas*, so indifferent to reason!

They would come to a village and inspect the cattle. They would examine the tongues and mouths of the finest yoke of oxen in Mexico. They would say: "These oxen have the sickness. They must be destroyed."

The owner of the oxen might cry out in protest, plead for mercy in tones of anguish; but there was no remedy.

Members of *La Comisión* would order a deep hole dug into the earth. If there were many cattle with the sickness, a great hole was dug with a great roaring machine called "the bulldozer." If the cattle were few, the hole might be small and dug with shovels. But the results were always the same. Into these holes the oxen were driven, mercilessly shot down by the "sanitary" rifles of the soldiers, and their bodies covered over.

Then a member of *La Comisión* would give money to the owner of the oxen and say: "Here is pay from the government for your

CERVEZA
CARTA BLANCA
EXQUISI
-Bill-

oxen. Keep this money, that you may buy mules to draw your plows. The hoof of a mule is not cloven; therefore he will not take the sickness. The mules will be brought within the near future."

"But, *señor,* I have not harness for mules; I have only the yoke for my dead oxen."

"The harness will be furnished. At no extra cost."

"But I know not the nature of a mule!"

"You will learn."

And The People did learn. They learned that the mule was an animal without patience. Beat him and curse him, and the beast fought back. He kicked and he bit. He took fright at all manner of foolish things and snorted and ran and tore down fences and wrecked harness and plows. And even when he was willing to follow the furrows, he walked too fast.

Ay! How one did pant, trying to keep up with the seedless beasts! How the sweat did pour! How one's legs did ache! How one did long for the slow, patient gait of oxen—the pace of Mexico!

Also there were times, after the oxen had been killed, when the mules were slow in arriving. Often, a fiesta day came first. And, for a fiesta, money is necessary. One says to himself: "I will spend only a very small part of the money received for my murdered oxen. There will still be enough left to buy mules."

So he spends a very small part of his money for wine. Then along come more thirsty friends, and he spends another small part. Then comes that reckless feeling of prosperity that goes with wine-drinking on fiesta days. Soon the mules are forgotten, the money is spent, and the one who once owned the finest yoke of oxen in Mexico sobers up in jail, with no oxen, no money, and no mules.

All because of *La Comisión*'s heartlessness and indifference to reason.

God's Own Little Pig

Near the village of Tiríndaro stood an ancient adobe-walled hut, roofed with short, overlapping sections of maguey blades. In the hut lived an Indian woman of so many years that The People called her "The Old One." With The Old One lived Chuchi, a spotted, long-snouted, diminutive pig.

The pig Chuchi filled that great place in the heart of The Old One left empty by the death of her man, by the loss of two sons to the army, and by the one daughter who worked in a *casa de putas* and seldom bothered to visit her mother.

Chuchi ate beans and tortillas with The Old One. At night he slept on the same floor mat, snuggling up against her withered breasts in a manner to remind her of that long-ago time when those breasts were full to bursting with milk for hungry babies. And any time of the day when Chuchi wandered from the hut, nuzzling for food among the cow droppings and garbage dumps of the village,

Bill

The Old One had only to call and Chuchi came, running and squealing, to rub against The Old One's spindly legs and utter little grunts of affection.

Chuchi was the one warm, living, breathing creature that stood between The Old One and the vast loneliness known to the old ones in every land.

Thus it was to be expected that when *La Comisión* came with its long and wicked needles The Old One rose up in defense of her beloved.

First she reasoned, then she pleaded, and finally, realizing the inevitable, she felt leap inside her a dark and terrible anger. Down from the low roof of the hut she snatched a scythe with a fresh-honed edge that glinted in the sunlight. Wheeling, she ran forward and placed herself between Chuchi and the soldiers. Standing there with the scythe raised threateningly, with her bare feet planted wide apart in the hot dust of Mexico's earth, she stared straight into the black bores of the rifles trained on her and cursed the soldiers and the gringos with a magnificent defiance.

"Dogs of dogs!" she charged them. "He-goats! Offspring of the Devil's whores! Would you murder God's own little pig?"

They would do even that!

While the soldiers, guns held ready, advanced upon her, a dog of a *matavaca* sneaked in from behind and snatched up the squealing Chuchi.

The Old One whirled with a scream of rage. The scythe flashed a bright arc in the sunlight. But a hard-swung rifle barrel deflected the deadly blow and chopped The Old One down, felling her to the earth, where her screams all but drowned out the gasping squeals of the terrified Chuchi as the long needle drove under his skin.

When The Old One finally struggled to her feet, *los matavacas* were already departing. She ran after them a way, shouting curses and obscenities through the dust kicked up by the rubber-tired wheels. Then, weeping brokenly, she returned to gather the beloved Chuchi into her arms and await his death.

By one of God's miracles, Chuchi lived, although for months afterward he wore a knot above one ear, a terrible knot, fully as large as one of The Old One's gnarled and broken-nailed thumbs.

What Is the Remedy for Death?

Such attitudes did some of the gringos hold! Such a blindness to the simple facts of life!

One came into a village in the hot district of Michoacán, his eyes round with amazement, his lips quivering with questions.

"I drove past this Mexican on a mountain road," the gringo exclaimed. "The man was driving one burro. Lying across this burro's back was another whose head the man bore on his shoulder. What was the meaning of such conduct? What does it signify?"

The interpretation was one of absolute simplicity. One of the man's beloved burros was infirm. The owner was merely assisting the poor creature to water or to his home where he might care for it.

"But how can this be?" the gringo persisted. "How can a Mexican be said to love his burros when he beats and curses them as he does his woman, when he allows them to die of hunger and disease?"

Such a question! A man beats his burro or his woman when they

become laggard. He allows them to go hungry because he is poor and has no food. If they die, it is because God wills it, and where is the remedy for death?

These are simple facts of life and have nothing to do with a man's capacity for love.

There Is Always Tomorrow

In Mexico, as all Mexicans know, there is always tomorrow, a much better time than today for performing whatever labors cannot be entirely avoided.

But apparently gringo members of *La Comisión* were completely unaware of this truth. Like men bitten by little ants, they drove furiously here and there, worked as if time could not wait, and had no respect for the siesta hour.

Also, at times, they were guilty of disturbing one's sleep with foolish and inconsiderate questions.

Consider the act of one called Eduardo Quiñónez, of Laredo, Texas. With such a name and such a birthplace, it would seem that he might understand The People. But this was not so.

On a sunny afternoon, as he drove his power wagon along a four-lane burro trail near the village of Pénjamo, he came upon a wide flat, devoid of trees. Out in the middle of this flat he saw a man asleep under his horse. The man had been careful to line up his horse

in such a manner that the animal's body shielded him completely from the burning rays of the sun. The man slept, sitting up, with his back resting comfortably against the insides of his horse's forelegs.

The horse slept, also.

What manner of barbarians must these gringos be to arouse a man from such peaceful slumbers, merely to ask foolish questions?

But this Eduardo Quiñónez did that very thing. He called to the sleeper and aroused him. "What passes, friend?" he asked. "Are you unable to sleep at night?"

"But, yes, *señor,*" the man said. "I sleep at night. Why not?"

"Then why must you sleep also in the daytime?"

The man sat in deep thought for a long moment. At last, a smile broke across his broad face and he said the thing that is always best to say when one is asked a foolish question: "*Quién sabe, señor?* Who knows?"

Then he leaned back against the horse's legs and resumed his slumbers.

These Are the Orders

Into Puruándiro came *La Comisión,* bringing the gringo vaccinators with their wicked needles. The captain gave orders to the local officials, who gave orders to the people.

"Bring your cattle down from the mountains," the *jefe* said. "Put them in corrals so that they may be picked with the needles. These are the orders."

So, with much labor, The People brought their livestock down from the mountains. They corralled them and watched fearfully as the vaccinators slammed the vicious needles into their innocent livestock. The People complained, but only to each other; and after awhile *La Comisión* went away.

But within four short months, *La Comisión* was back again, bringing more gringos and more needles. The gringos insisted that the cattle be picked again.

This was too much. The People said, "Why must the gringos be forever picking our cattle with their needles?"

The *jefe* said to *La Comisión:* "No, we will not corral the cattle

-Bill-

again, even for inspection. No, if your gringos are so desirous of picking animals with their needles, let them seek other animals in other parts."

Members of *La Comisión* argued. They explained that it was necessary to vaccinate all the cattle of the infected region every four months in order to maintain their immunity to the sickness. They said that if the cattle were not vaccinated again, they still might die.

The local *jefes* listened but were adamant. No. There would be no more picking of The People's animals at Puruándiro.

Gringos Les Hall and Dave Brown went to army Lieutenant Cárdenas and explained the situation.

Lieutenant Cárdenas listened and nodded. "It is of no consequence, *señores,*" he assured them. "I will persuade them."

Lieutenant Cárdenas went at once and arrested all the officials of Puruándiro. He took them to Tacámbaro, where he locked them in jail.

Four days later, the humbled officials were persuaded. They sent word to Lieutenant Cárdenas. When he came, they said, "Now we are ready to work with the gringos."

In the meantime, however, word came that an ambush was being prepared at a certain bend of the road leading back to Puruándiro. It was told that The People would waylay and shoot members of *La Comisión* when it came again.

When Lieutenant Cárdenas learned of this, he once more assured the gringos, "It is of no consequence. I will persuade them."

Then the lieutenant ordered out twelve of his soldiers to accompany *La Comisión.* He armed them with rifles and put them aboard the power wagon. Aboard the same power wagon he placed the released officials of Puruándiro, one in the cab with Hall, and one on each side, on the machine's running boards.

He gave orders to the soldiers. "If the officials step from the machine, shoot them. If you are fired upon, shoot first the officials."

13-476
3
1646
-Bill-

They were not fired upon.

And when *La Comisión* arrived at Puruándiro, the *jefe* called The People together.

"Bring your cattle down from the mountains," he said. "Corral them, that the gringos may pick them with their needles. These are the orders. There is no remedy."

A Roper of Uncommon Ability

To Zinapécuaro, where members of *La Comisión* picked the cattle, came a diminutive vaquero known as The Small One. He came with soft, eager eyes and a consuming desire to assist the gringos in their work.

He said to the inspector: "I, *señor,* am a roper of uncommon ability. Witness the condition of my *reata.*"

He held up for inspection a hard-twist rope of maguey fiber known as the *reata de pita,* one so knotted and frayed by hard usage that the inspector was instantly convinced that only a roper of uncommon ability could catch anything with it.

But the offer of assistance in a region where the work of *La Comisión* was met with sullen resistance called for indulgence. The inspector nodded.

The Small One moved into the milling, bawling herd. He selected a huge bull and made his cast.

The loop settled about the bull's horns. Other vaqueros tied onto the rope with The Small One. Together they dragged the plunging animal to a snubbing post, where they tied him securely.

But the strength of the bull was such that one sudden twist of his mighty head broke the frayed rope.

"*Madre de Dios!*" cried The Small One in consternation. "The great beast has broken the only *reata* I possess!"

He turned to the inspector, spreading limp and upturned palms to demonstrate the extent of the calamity.

"*Señor,*" he said, "I am informed that you possess a *reata* like none to be found in Mexico. One woven from the fibers of silk and of incredible strength and flexibility. Is it possible that you would favor me with the loan of it? Otherwise, I am helpless to continue with the work."

The inspector went to the power wagon. He brought out a new silk rope that he had had sent down from Texas after learning that the ropes furnished by *La Comisión* lacked the strength to hold the heavier bulls. He handed it to The Small One, whose eyes grew round with wonder at the white beauty of it.

"*Cristo Santo!*" cried The Small One. "What a miracle of construction!" He turned to the others. "Observe the feel of it. How smooth to the touch! How firm and alive! Like the flesh of a strong young woman!"

Before the others had a chance to observe the feel of the silk *reata,* however, The Small One whirled toward the herd, exclaiming, "With such a *reata,* it is impossible to miss! Allow me to demonstrate."

And he did so. In his hands, the new silk rope became a live thing that hissed and sang as the loop leaped through the air with deadly accuracy. Not once did the loop miss its target, even at the longest cast.

Nor was there a bull in the herd with the strength to break it.

-Bill-

Huge bulls, great *bravos* from the mountain, threw their full weight against it and were helpless.

All vaqueros present agreed that this was a *reata superior,* and all agreed that it was a cruel stroke of fate that the gringo owner should lose it.

But accidents will occur, even to a roper of uncommon ability.

The work with the needle was done. The corral gates were flung open. The harassed cattle were stampeding for the open when The Small One attempted to remove the loop of the inspector's new rope from the horns of the last bull.

Was it his fault that at that very instant the impatient bull made a dash for freedom? Was he to be blamed for not gripping tighter a rope that was running through his bare hands at such a speed as to burn them like a hot iron? Did he not run after the bull, shouting and waving his hands, calling on the recalcitrant beast to halt? Was he not still chasing after the bull when the animal led him out of sight of the corrals?

Only an outraged gringo, bitter at the loss of a new silk *reata,* would have been so unkind as to suggest that The Small One was a "Goddam thief who aimed to steal my rope from the start!"

Now They Are Shooting The People!

Even the dogs of the ranches resented the coming of *La Comisión*.

The dogs were the protectors of the flocks. They guarded the goats and sheep and chickens and pigs from marauding coyotes and eagles. They were seldom fed and therefore accustomed to foraging for their food as do the buzzards and other scavengers of Mexico. They were lean and hungry dogs and very savage. They took fierce delight in biting any member of *La Comisión* who dared set foot within their domain.

The gringos fought back. They beat the dogs with sticks. They tried to run them down with their jeeps and power wagons. They often roped the dogs for the sport of watching their wild antics on the end of a rope.

To remove their ropes, the gringos would clamp a pig *narigón* over the dog's nose to hold his mouth shut while they slipped off the noose. But much as they feared and resented the rope and muzzle

Bill

treatment, many dogs, after being released, would attack a second time.

One dog was so persistent in his savage attacks that at last gringo Bill Leftwich ordered a soldier to shoot it.

News of this killing spread swiftly across the ranches and grew into a rumor of far worse deeds. By the time Leftwich had driven to the adjoining village, The People were crying out to each other in alarm, "*La Comisión* is now shooting The People!"

Many, fearing for their lives, were already fleeing into the mountains.

With a Gun to Clear the Way

There was one gringo who, it was said, came to resent *La Comisión* he worked for almost as much as did The People.

This one did not fear the needle; it was told that he had even submitted himself to be picked by similar ones. He did not resent the hard work *La Comisión* demanded of him. He was a *Tejano* who all his life had worked hard in the cattle country around Cotulla, Texas. The thing that eventually became intolerable to him was the conflicting orders of too many in authority and the stupid changes that were forever being made in the official papers he was required to fill out.

This one had worked long and hard in the vicinity of Ojuelos, in the northeastern tip of Jalisco. He worked under an investigator, sent there to examine cattle for blisters on their tongues and gums, one symptom of the sickness.

For the length of two weeks, the *Tejano* roped and wrestled and

-Bill-

dragged heavy bulls and wild steers to the snubbing posts and tied them solidly, so the inspector might be safe from their wicked horns. He pried open the steers' mouths, pulled out their long tongues, and held them out until the inspector could make his examination. And this heavy work was all done during the dry season, when the sun's heat was at its fiercest, when the corral dust, churned up by the cattle's hooves, rose and hung about a man's head in a choking, blinding cloud. And not one time did this *Tejano* lag at the work or voice a single word of complaint.

But at last, dirty and bone-weary, he returned to the district office at Irapuato in Guanajuato. There he presented to the paymaster the official claim forms. These were papers he had filled out with great care and painful endeavor, in order to receive reimbursement for his own money spent on horses, hay, food, and other items needed to accomplish the work.

The paymaster was one from California who felt himelf a superior to those who sweated. He glanced at the papers, then flung them contemptuously back to the *Tejano.*

"The forms have been changed while you were away. I cannot pay until new ones have been filled out properly."

As the *Tejano* tried to explain later, the *Californiano*'s mistake was not in the words he spoke but in their manner of delivery.

The anger of the *Tejano* was that of a man who lives in a hot country—quick and dangerous. He reached for the revolver that he wore at his side. He lifted and shoved it into the face of the paymaster. He said: "They told me to collect from you, and, by God, I aim to collect! Now!"

And he collected.

But he still was not satisfied. He still resented the number of times he had been ordered to do one thing by one in charge, only to have those orders changed by some other official of equal rank. He could not forget all the hours he had spent licking his pencil point and worrying his brains sick, trying to fill out in duplicate the senseless official forms, only to have them rejected when presented for payment. Added to this was the irritation of having others who worked for *La Comisión* tell him how unwise he had been to persuade that paymaster with a gun.

"The hell with it!" he exclaimed. "I'm catching a morning train and heading straight for Texas. Where you work under one single wagon boss and they ain't no papers to fill out."

"But you can't," the others protested. "You're employed by Civil Service. You'll have to go to Mexico City first to sign out, to turn in your equipment, to clear your passport."

"The hell I can't," the *Tejano* declared impatiently. "If you don't think I'm catching me a train bound straight for Texas, you just come down in the morning and watch me buy a ticket."

And when he boarded the train the following morning, those who watched felt certain that he would arrive at Cotulla, Texas, without delay.

For, as The People pointed out, it is very difficult to prevent a homesick *Tejano* from returning to his country when he is possessed of a gun to clear the way.

-Bill-

The Private and His Gun

For a soldier in the Mexican Army, especially for the private, the coming of *La Comisión* was an added hardship.

His orders would come down through the higher ranks. Then he would go to his woman and say, "Prepare to leave. We go to Morelia."

And the woman would say, "But to Morelia is more than fifty kilometers."

"That is of no consequence. Were it one hundred kilometers, we would still go. I have my orders."

So the woman would saddle the soldier's horse and to the saddle attach all their belongings: a charcoal brazier, cooking utensils, blankets, sleeping mats, food, parrots, laying hens, fighting roosters, and children. Then she would climb into the saddle and say, "We are prepared."

And the soldier, carrying his rifle across one shoulder and a bandoleer of cartridges across the other, would catch up the bridle reins and lead the horse on the long walk to Morelia.

Arriving there, he would seek quarters for his woman and children in some church, the same church into which were crowded the women and children of other soldiers, often so many that three and four families occupied floor space of no more than twelve by twelve feet. That the church was old and damp and cold, with water seeping down the faces of the crumbling walls, was a matter of little concern. It was no worse and no better than the last building that had served as barracks.

Leaving his wife to select quarters for them among the bustling and noisy confusion of chattering women, quacking ducks, squealing pigs, and shrieking children, the soldier went in search of the nearest cantina. Along the way, he closely observed where and how one might most easily come into possession of a goat, a sack of beans, green corn, or ripening squash.

For after a soldier has bought a little wine to quench his thirst and marijuana to help him forget, and has possibly bet too much on the wrong rooster, it is not to be expected that he will have money left with which to buy food. Not on a private's pay of four pesos and sixty-three centavos a day. No, he must employ other means to provide for himself and his family. And in a new town, the devious acquisition of food is often no easy accomplishment.

Still, there were certain compensations in being attached to *La Comisión*. A salary increase of one peso a day bought extra wine and marijuana. To ride about the country in a roaring power wagon was no little pleasure. But greatest of all was the honor of being issued a new rifle, a modern bolt-action Mauser still encased in the packing grease.

To the Mexican soldier, the acquisition of a new gun upon which no other soldier had ever laid a hand was like gaining the consent of a virgin.

-Bill-

He cleaned his gun. He fondled it lovingly. He marveled at its beauty. He all but inserted a cartridge and fired it—but, of course, when a soldier has to account for every cartridge issued and pay to the army one peso for every one fired or missing, he tends to control any rash urge toward indiscriminate shooting.

But with the new rifle came a new pride to the soldier, so that he performed his duties with zeal and alertness. And without him, the work of *La Comisión* would have failed.

Even several of the proud, arrogant, and often contemptuous *Tejanos* have said this of him.

Is a Trooper Made of Iron?

Consider the truly tragic experience of a certain corporal of the Fourteenth Cavalry, quartered at Morelia.

The sergeant said to the corporal: "You will ride to Villa Madero. The cavalry escort for *La Comisión* has not been paid in two months. You will deliver their pay."

Now, from Morelia to Villa Madero is a long and tiresome day's journey, even in the dry season. In the wet season, as it was then, it is an almost impossible ride. The trails are wet and slippery. There are dangerously flooded streams to be forded. The rain pours down, wetting and chilling one to the very marrow of his bones.

Was it to be expected that even a brave corporal of the Fourteenth Cavalry make such a ride in such weather without seeking what small comforts as could be purchased at the various cantinas along the way?

True, the money he spent was not his money. Yet which of the corporal's fellow-troopers, comfortable in his dry quarters at Villa Madero, could find it in his soul to begrudge a tiny portion of his pay for so worthy a cause? Without wine to give the corporal strength, he might never complete the journey, might never deliver the money.

For truly this journey was an arduous one, made exceedingly more difficult by the horse the corporal rode. Was ever a Mexican trooper mounted upon a beast so stupid, one with so little ability to keep his feet under him? Let the corporal sway in his saddle but the slightest as he lifted a wine jug to his lips, and out the horse's feet would fly and down into the mud they would go. Invariably, as the horse scrambled to his feet, he trampled upon the fallen trooper, bruising him and tracking his uniform with mud. Often many precious drops of wine were spilled, to soak into the mud where they could be recovered by no man.

Is a trooper made of iron? Can he endure forever such cruel punishment? No. Even the patience of a corporal has its limits.

When the horse fell again in the bottom of a deep and muddy canyon, pinning the corporal's leg under his threshing body, then rising to stamp unmercifully upon his rider, the corporal unslung his rifle. He took careful aim. He shot the clumsy beast between the eyes.

It was only two days later that, footsore and weary, he arrived at Villa Madero. He still had his saddle and blanket and bridle. He still had his rifle. He even had some of the payroll money left.

But would the soldiers allow him to tell of the dangers he had faced, the untold miseries he had endured, the toil and trouble and great sacrifice that had been necessary to bring them their money?

No! In their greed and stupidity, they became angry that the money, when apportioned, amounted to only five pesos each. They reported to the sergeant, and the sergeant was enraged by the shooting of that stupid horse and came and beat the poor corporal so un-

-Bill-

mercifully with his fists that the captain put the sergeant under arrest for thirty days.

As if that were not enough, the troopers jeered at the corporal. They asked him if, by shooting his horse, he was attempting to transfer to the infantry.

And on top of all the other indignities, now, at each payday, the poor soldier must endure having the major portion of his pay taken from him, that it might be applied to the cost of a horse, the cost of a wasted cartridge, and a bar bill to the amount of five hundred pesos.

All that to come from the pay of a corporal!

A Fighter Far from Home

Attached to *La Comisión* was one Lieutenant Cárdenas. He was a Yaqui Indian from the state of Sonora, and he was a fighter.

All Yaquis are fighters. This is a fact readily attested to by those who recall the Mexican Army's many bloody failures to drive the Yaquis from their traditional homeland in northern Mexico.

Joined now with that same Mexican Army, Lieutenant Cárdenas served with the knowledge that should he fall in battle his soul would return to dwell among the high wild mountains of Sonora and Chihuahua. This is a knowledge that gives strength and comfort to all Yaqui soldiers who fight far from home.

No soldier attached to *La Comisión* was more alert and faithful to his duties than Lieutenant Cárdenas. All the gringos agreed to this, even Les Hall, from Uvalde, Texas, whom the lieutenant once tried to kill.

The lieutenant would tolerate no delays in the work of *La Comisión*. He was quick to step between the gringos and any who resented and sought to harm them. Should a soldier in his command become drunk and slack in his duties, that one was brought to account in such a manner as to leave a lasting impression on his mind.

For example, there was the time the lieutenant came upon this soldier who had fallen into a drunken sleep while on guard.

The lieutenant called for his sergeant and said: "Place a guard over this soldier. He wishes to rest."

So a guard was placed over the sleeper, and for forty-eight hours he lay and rested.

A jungle storm blew up at midnight, all but drowning him. At noon the next day, the heat of the sun bore down upon his reclining body with an intensity that all but roasted him. Yet not one time did he so much as raise his head. For over him, all this time, stood the guard with a rifle pointed at his head and with orders to make sure that the soldier's rest was completed.

Yet, when not on duty, the lieutenant liked his drink as well as any other soldier. And that is how, at Zacapú, in Michoacán, he came into trouble.

It was payday and the lieutenant was off duty. So he drank at this cantina and at that one until he became extremely sociable. At this point, he encountered Les Hall, Hall's partner, and Dr. Alvarado, a Mexican veterinarian. Filled with the love of all mankind, the lieutenant fell upon the three, insisting that they come at once and drink with him.

Dr. Alvarado and Hall's partner accepted with the graciousness of true gentlemen. But Hall, for all the respect he held for the lieutenant as a soldier, was wary of him as a social drinker. So he began making excuses. And to one as far along in his cups as the lieutenant, the excuses sounded thin.

And when he caught Hall slipping away and climbing into the

4
-Bill-

cab of his truck, Lieutenant Cárdenas knew that he had been insulted. And to a lieutenant of the Mexican Army, full of the fierce pride of his Yaqui forebears, such an insult was not a thing to be taken lightly.

In hot anger, the lieutenant drew his pistol and fired at Hall. But such was his fortune that the truck was already moving, so that the bullet wasted its force tearing through the metal parts of the cab.

Still, there was some satisfaction to be had in seeing how swiftly the frightened gringo raced his truck around a street corner. That, and how quickly all the people strolling along the streets melted away at the sound of the shot.

Laughing to himself, the lieutenant entered a nearby cantina, where he ordered another drink. And it was there that the fat little army major who worked with the local police found him and ordered him to throw down his pistol.

Which was a very foolish order, considering the well-known fact that a Mexican officer cherishes his pistol almost as much as his life.

When the lieutenant reached for his pistol, he did not throw it down. Instead, he buried the muzzle of it deep in the folds of the major's paunch and informed him that no "steer belly" got his gun.

This act so terrified the major that he wheeled and raced out of the cantina and through the darkening streets shouting "*Policía! Policía!*"

The lieutenant turned to his unfinished drink. He was still partaking of it when the police arrived.

The policemen allowed him to stare into the little black eyes of their rifles for a moment, then asked, "Do you submit to arrest?"

The lieutenant considered. Finally, he said, "Only if allowed to retain my pistol."

Now the policemen considered, but not for long. They understood a soldier's passionate love for his pistol.

"Agreed," they said.

6-TOROS-6
3oo SOL
5cc SOMBRA
ACAPU
-Bill-

So the lieutenant allowed himself to be arrested and spent the rest of the night and the next day in jail, still wearing his pistol.

Hall did his best to persuade the fat major not to report Lieutenant Cárdenas, but his efforts were wasted. The report went through, and as a result the finest and most helpful soldier ever attached to *La Comisión* was transferred to the hot coastal zone dreaded by all soldiers, where, according to gringo Tom Roberts, the mosquitoes were of a size to necessitate their drinking from horse troughs.

The Spent Cartridge

Chief of the Mexican inspectors for *La Comisión* in District III was the proud and fierce Colonel Carlos Borjás Ramos, ranchero of Chihuahua and strong man of Mexican politics.

Colonel Ramos performed two valuable services for *La Comisión*: he made possible the almost instant release of any member of *La Comisión* who was sobering up in jail, and he provided excellent and unending entertainment by relating tales of his adventures as a soldier of *La Revolución*.

His advice to members of *La Comisión* on how best to get along with his countrymen was simple and to the point: "Always carry a gun, and shoot first."

"For," he explained, "I can get you out of jail, my friend, but to get you out of the cemetery is an impossibility."

And get them out of the jails he would. The jailers might make sly remarks about the colonel to his back, such as calling him *El*

Cartucho Quemado, "The Spent Cartridge," because of his extreme age and inclination to speak always of *La Revolución.* But never once did they argue when he appeared at a jail door, drew his revolver, and spoke with the true pride and arrogance of a Mexican Army commander:

"I am Colonel Ramos. You hold prisoner a member of *La Comisión.* He needs to be at work. Release him—at once!"

The gringo prisoner might be charged with drunkenness, with fighting, with shooting out windowpanes all over town—that was of no consequence. He was released—at once—and all charges were dropped.

For, despite his age and his garrulous tongue, the colonel was *muy hombre.* None could deny this. Had he not fought on *both* sides of *La Revolución?* Listen to his tale, told with affluence in the English, of which he is now the master:

"Comes the Revolution, and I know this Pancho Villa from the days when he is merely a hired vaquero; therefore I join the *Federalistas.* But in a battle, I am captured, along with eighty of my *compañeros.* We prisoners are stood against an adobe wall and are being shot by *Villistas* when there occurs a miracle. I am recognized by my godfather, a commander in Villa's army. My godfather removes me from the line and takes me to Pancho Villa. Villa say: 'I give you a choice, Don Carlos Borjás Ramos. Fight with me—or go back and join your late friends at the wall.'

"Being no political fanatic, I bow slightly, but with dignity. I say, 'I shall be happy to serve you, my general.'

"Then Villa points a finger at me and say, 'You are a colonel in my army.'

"So now, I am a 'finger' colonel of the *Villistas,* and I fight the *Federalistas* for two years. I receive two grave wounds—from a bullet of the caliber .30 that pierces my leg, and from a burst of shrapnel that breaks my collarbone.

"Then my military career comes to a climax near the American border. We are routed by an overpowering force of *Federalistas*. Some run this way. I do not like that way, therefore I run this other direction.

"After I ride a long time, I see three United States soldiers on horses; so I hide in a canyon until they are gone, then ride a long time more.

"Soon, I arrive to Douglas, Arizona. A bus stops near me, and I get on. The man asks me for a ticket, but I do not yet speak the English. Therefore, I smile and offer him money.

" 'To Tucson?' he asks.

" 'To Tucson,' I say.

"So I ride to Tucson and live in these United States for twenty-three years. And my godfather is wounded to death in a battle and Pancho Villa is killed after *La Revolución;* but now I am returned to Mexico, still alive, and with a fine cattle ranch in the state of Chihuahua.

"Is that not a fine adventure for a man to have lived, my friend?"

Allow Me to Demonstrate

Sent along on this morning to guard gringo Herb Prescott and his vaccinating brigade were soldiers of the Fourteenth Cavalry Regiment. The night before, these soldiers had participated in a fiesta celebration the like of which had seldom been heard of in that part of Mexico. Such dancing! Such beautiful and willing women! Such an abundance of wine! Even yet, hours after the finish of the celebration, many of the soldiers were still so full of exuberance and swagger they could hardly contain themselves.

One stood inside a corral and watched Herb Prescott waste a loop on a Brahma steer he had meant to catch. In disgust, the soldier grabbed up a rope from the corral dust.

"Make room!" he shouted. "Allow me to demonstrate to this gringo the proficiency of a true vaquero of Mexico!"

The steer raced past. The soldier's loop leaped through the air

with the speed and accuracy of a striking snake. With a shout of triumph, the soldier jerked closed the loop about the Brahma's horns.

But the Brahma was large and full of power. To hold him, the soldier was required to exert great force. In the ensuing struggle, the soldier's blood rushed to his head, bringing with it much of the wine consumed the night before. This caused dizziness and confusion, so that the soldier allowed the rifle slung across his shoulders to slide down about his waist, pinning his arms to his sides. At the same instant, his trousers slipped from his waist to gather about his ankles.

What a shame! What an indignity! What an inglorious end to a brave attempt to uphold the honor of Mexico!

The wine-washed brain of the soldier refused to accept the calamity. It slipped into a state of complete oblivion. The soldier pitched face forward into the corral dust. There he lay in the hot sun all day, not even flinching when kicked and stepped on by the frightened cattle trying to escape the gringo's loop.

At sundown, when *La Comisión* prepared to leave the corral, two of the soldier's companions came and picked him up by his shirt and sagging pants and loaded him on the truck.

By the time they had arrived back in town, however, the soldier had recovered.

"It is said," he observed with eager anticipation, "that tonight's celebration will be of even greater gaiety."

Gringos Are Wild Men

The Aftosa gringos were wild men. They were demented. It was impossible to think otherwise.

Consider how, at the annual fiesta at Villa Madero, Preston Dillon and Wade Miller originated a contest between themselves for no other purpose than to defy death.

Before the very eyes of those who came to watch the roping and riding, these wild gringos rode their horses close together, so that each could tie one end of the same rope to his saddle horn. Then they swung their mounts about, so that they stood rump to rump.

The People stared in bewilderment. Had the gringos lost their senses? Had they suddenly become bitter enemies? They had arrived at the fiesta together, riding side by side as friends; but when the *charanda* flows freely, tempers sometimes flare. And then, of course, there is always the possibility of a woman. . . .

But no, both men were laughing. And they were still laughing when the signal was given and both set spurs to their horses.

The horses dashed apart. The rope between them leaped from the earth and straightened. The inevitable occurred.

One horse was hauled over backward. He and Preston Dillon struck the ground with all six feet in the air!

But the rider slid to safety, plowing a long furrow in the dusty cow dung of the corral with the back of his head.

He sprang instantly to his feet, still shouting his laughter.

Truly, such a contest was only for crazy men or drunken fools.

Yet, to witness such daring, to hear such rollicking laughter in the face of death, is to feel yourself in the presence of a certain magnificence.

It is impossible to think otherwise!

Patachica

What a man was Tom Roberts, this inspector for *La Comisión* who came to be called *Patachica* because of his tiny feet.

On fiesta days, he would attend the rodeos and ride the fiercest of the untamed bulls and horses. Ride them as if the feat were nothing, barely holding with one hand to the twisted-grass *soga* tied around the animal's body. Ride them and spur them and chew and spit while he did it.

"*Carne seca,*" he told The People when first they inquired what class of food he chewed so constantly.

But they knew that this was not so. Dried meat does not stimulate such a flow of mouth juices as to enable a man to expectorate from one side of a wide road to the other. Nor will dried meat, no matter how well masticated or thickly applied, stain the whole polished side of a power wagon such a rich chocolate brown.

No, it had to be something else.

So strong was the puzzled ones' curiosity and so diligent were they with inquiry and constant observation that finally they outsmarted *Patachica* and learned the astonishing truth. Only to be more puzzled than ever.

It was tobacco that he chewed!

They shook their heads. They argued. Some absolutely refused to believe it. They discussed the matter for days. Finally they came to accept it as a fact, but that it was a habit was incomprehensible to them.

Everybody in Mexico *smoked* tobacco. But who, besides a wild *Tejano* from San Antonio, would *chew* it? And chew it so constantly!

Consider the time he attempted to ford the Río de las Balsas, that wild mountain stream dividing the states of Michoacán and Guerrero.

He came in his power wagon, and one who knew the country rode with him to direct him across the stream.

The guide said, "To keep safely in the shallow water, you will go directly toward that tree on the opposite bank."

So *Patachica* drove his power wagon into the water, going directly toward the tree, and fell into a hole so deep that the nose of the power wagon went under. And he swore and pushed open the cab door and leaped out. And his guide pushed open the opposite door to escape in that direction. And, with both doors shoved open, the main current of the Río de las Balsas came flooding through, taking with it a leather briefcase containing many hundreds of pesos that *Patachica* had brought along to buy horses and saddles and food and whatever else *La Comisión* might need for efficient operation in the mountains.

Fortunately the leather case floated, and *Patachica* saw it and dived after. The strong current caught him and rolled him over and beat him against the rocks. But he struggled mightily and swam

strongly and at last rescued the case and fought his way to the safety of the bank. There, almost drowned, he finally had time to pucker his lips and spit the greatest and brownest spurt of tobacco juice ever to stain the banks of the wild-running Río de las Balsas!

Ay! Muy hombre, that *Patachica,* that gringo chewer of tobacco!

Nearly Mexican

There was a time, when first he came to the town of Acuitzio del Canje, in the state of Michoacán, that *Patachica,* the gringo *Tejano* of the little feet and the big tobacco chew, was resented by The People. This came about because of his strange attitude toward women. As unbelievable as it may seem, he thought a woman was a man's equal!

An honest, hard-working, perfectly respectable farmer might be going into town to deliver a load of hay. And his woman, upon whose shoulders the hay was being transported, might be indolent that morning, so that a man in a hurry would find it necessary to apply the whip.

Consider then this man's surprise and consternation when suddenly the whip is jerked from his hand and he is assaulted by a furious gringo whose huge balled fists strike with the weight of sledge hammers.

"But, *señor!*" the man cries out in protest, "why do you assault me?"

"For whipping the woman!"

"But she is *my* woman."

"That gives you no right to whip her!"

How is a man to answer such a preposterous assertion? If a man does not have the right to whip his own woman, who has that right? A woman is like a burro; when she grows lazy, the whip must be applied. How else could a man expect to get work out of either?

But to try to explain this to the new inspector of *La Comisión* was hopeless. He would not listen. And if a man became angry and attempted to fight back against this injustice, he got the long barrel of a .45 revolver shoved deep into his belly.

And only a fool argues with a gun.

So it was to be expected that after several of these outrageous infringements on their rights, the men of Acuitzio came to resent the gringo Tom Roberts.

They made known their resentment in many ways. They turned their backs on him when he walked past. They very obviously did not offer to buy him a drink when he entered a cantina. If he asked the way to some ranch in the mountains, they directed him in the opposite direction. In his hearing, one and then another made sly speculations about what manner of life *Americanos* must lead in a land where the woman carries the whip.

But gradually, this gringo with the small feet came to learn what every stranger in a strange land comes eventually to learn—that Mexico is Mexico and Texas is Texas, and the man who wishes to live in either must learn to accept the customs of the people.

Then came September 16, the *gran fiesta* day for all of Mexico. And on this same day, *Patachica* learned still another thing—that the girl in Texas he planned to marry was entering a convent to become a nun.

This was a crushing blow to the young gringo. To assuage his hurt, he plied himself with strong drink and rode through town on a

MORELIA
PLAZA

half-wild, mouse-colored mountain mule, shooting off his revolvers as often as any of the Mexican fiesta-day celebrants.

Then, after darkness had shut down and the cantinas were the fullest and the revelry was at its highest peak of action, the broken-hearted *Tejano* of the small feet did such a bold and daring deed that no man in the village could do less than show him the greatest respect and admiration.

He spurred his mouse-colored mule into the largest cantina in town, pulled his guns, and, without missing one shot, shattered every electric light bulb in the place.

It was the duty of the local police to arrest him, of course, and the officers did make some show of trying to catch him as he spurred out of town into the darkness. But after he had been hidden out in the mountains for three days, some woodcutters brought him the news that the police had given up the search. As the woodcutters explained it, even a gringo who celebrated September 16 with such zeal as to shoot out seven electric light bulbs without a miss was *casi Mejicano.*

So the rejected suitor returned to Acuitzio, to find himself one of the most respected men in town. Citizens felt honored to be allowed to buy him a drink. They invited him to participate in hunts for coyotes and doves and quail. They called on him to attend all important meetings of the town officials and were most insistent that he ride at the head of every fiesta-day parade.

And those whom he had once assaulted for whipping their women laughed in warm remembrance. After all, he was only an ignorant *Tejano* then. Now, he was *casi Mejicano!*

The Woman of Mexico

To gringo members of *La Comisión,* the prodigious and unceasing toil of the woman of Mexico was beyond comprehension, almost beyond belief.

She milked the goats, fed the cattle, ground the corn, butchered the pigs, gathered the wood, carried the water, wove the blankets, washed the clothes, swept the floors, dug the potatoes, strung the peppers, patched the fences, reaped the wheat, plowed the fields, stripped the cane, gathered the fruit, delivered the produce to market, cared for the sick, bore the children, and at night on the mat gave comfort and release to her man.

These duties and many more she performed daily, with the patience and fortitude of one prepared to accept life on the terms that God wills, gracefully and without complaint.

It was this quality in her nature that compelled the respect and admiration of every perceptive gringo. It was this quality that caused some to pause and reflect upon the nature of the women in

-Bill-

their own country—women who too often seemed to regard a life of ease not as a luxury to be grateful for but as a right to be demanded of their men.

It was this same quality that caused many young and unattached gringo members to ask themselves, "Why return to the States and become the slave of a woman when I can remain in Mexico and have a woman for my slave?"

The answer, of course, was obvious to any man except a fool.

The Bite

Gringo members of *La Comisión* were men of great skill and ability. None could deny this fact. They had attended the schools and acquired much useful knowledge. They could read the books. They could fill out papers in such a manner that the government would pay them well. They could repair a broken rifle, make a balky jeep engine run, and often had skill with the medicines.

Yet, there were times when they revealed such an ignorance of simple matters that it was truly astonishing.

For example. In a lake called Pátzcuaro, in the state of Michoacán, there is an island called Jarácuaro. To this island the rancheros often swim their herds, that the cattle may graze and grow fat upon the lush grass growing there.

To this island, in a small boat, came the gringo Bill Leftwich, with his second man, to pick cattle for the sickness.

The first animal to be snared by Leftwich's loop was a *bravo,*

-Bill-

a wild and recalcitrant steer from the mountains. He had great strength, this *bravo* did, and great spirit, as well as great stubbornness. He snorted and ran and kicked and bawled and fought until the gringos finally succeeded in throwing a hitch over the snubbing post. Then he balked. He stood with his four feet braced and refused to allow his head to be drawn up against the post and tied.

Yet this had to be done. For only a fool would attempt to stick a needle into the neck of an angry *bravo* with horns as wicked as drawn sabers and with the ability to kick a tick off his nose with either hind foot.

So, one gringo continued to pull on the rope while the other twisted the *bravo*'s tail and swore great oaths and whipped him with a braided rawhide whip and sweated and swore some more. And still the stubborn one held his feet in his tracks.

At last the one called Leftwich lost patience. He kicked the steer, driving a boot into the stubborn one's belly with such force and violence that tears came into his eyes and he all but fainted with the pain of his injured big toe.

Not until then did one of the herdsmen step forward to say, with true vaquero politeness, "*Señor,* if it is your wish, I will favor him with the bite."

"The bite?" Leftwich asked. "I do not understand the bite."

"It is a simple method that we vaqueros use," the man said, "but it has a certain value."

"If it will move that steer, it will have great value," Leftwich declared.

The vaquero nodded. "With your permission, *señor,*" he said.

Then he caught up the tail of the steer and bit down hard upon it with white and smiling teeth.

To the watching vaqueros, the *bravo's* bellow of pain and his sudden leap forward lacked the merit of surprise. They had expected it. What astonished them was the expressions that came into the faces of the gringos as the bellowing steer, head lowered and tongue protruding from his mouth, rushed toward the snubbing post.

So startled was the second man that he barely remembered in time to take up the slack in his rope before the pain-maddened *bravo* had charged past.

"Why, that's better than a hot-shot!" exclaimed Leftwich in admiration.

The vaqueros inquired into the nature of this "hot-shot." Upon learning that it was a prod pole charged with electricity, they envisioned it, considered its possibilities, and finally discarded it with shrugs of the shoulders.

Of what value, they asked themselves, is the invention of a machine that can accomplish no more than a man's bite?

The Man Who Smokes Like a Chimney

It must be admitted that among the gringos attached to *La Comisión* were some who in every way proved themselves true *caballeros*. They spoke the language, softly and with exactitude. If they violated a custom, it was only through ignorance, and they were quick to learn. They drank quietly and not too much, showed courtesy to women, and were fair in their dealings with men.

But such could not be said of the *Tejano* of the beer belly, the one who smoked with such constancy that he came to be called *El Hombre Que Fuma Como una Chimenea.*

He was of the "superior race." He was convinced that God, in giving him a skin of such slight pigmentation that the Mexico sun burned his face to the redness of a beet, had also given him the divine right to abuse and insult all whose skins were darker.

He was brutal and contemptuous of the Mexican woman he took to his bed in place of the wife he had left in Texas. In the cantinas, he drank heavily and alone and often paid for his drinks with vicious

-Bill-

insults. He had not even the decency to remove his spurs upon entering a stranger's house. As inspector for *La Comisión,* he employed curses for explanations.

So vile was the abuse that he heaped upon a number of rancheros at a corral in the *municipio* of Guanajuato that he was told: "You will go now. And should you return, you will be shot!"

This warning was given in a manner to convince him of its validity, and he went. For, although he knew himself to be superior, he was not at all certain that this superiority would turn a bullet. And never again would he return to that village.

Other gringos who worked with *La Comisión,* and who had almost as little use as the Mexicans for The Man Who Smokes Like a Chimney, learned of the incident and made sport out of attempting to devise ways of luring him back to this village. Their efforts failed, however; The Man continued to avoid the village, often riding miles out of his way to reach some place beyond.

Even more often, he went far out of his way to show his contempt for The People, so that they came to loathe and hate him and to pray for some miracle of ill fortune to befall him.

At last it did, in such a manner to bring smiles of glee to all who had known him. He stole a horse that spoke English!

The horse was called "Shorty" by the gringos. He belonged to *La Comisión* but was the pet of the wild and laughing Wade Miller, who rode him on inspection trips into the mountains outside Villa Madero.

Wade liked to get drunk and startle strangers with the information that "I've got the only horse in Mexico that can speak English." Then, when the strangers seemed doubtful, he liked to lead them out to the corrals and prove it.

He would enter the gate and call to Shorty, and Shorty would come. He would then talk to Shorty and pat him and romp with him. And Shorty, more like a dog than a horse, would play with him.

Then Wade would say to the strangers, "Now, observe this," and turn to Shorty and say, "Shorty, you old son of a bitch!"

Instantly, Shorty would take exception to this gringo obscenity. He would lay back his ears in anger, bare his teeth, run at his master, and try to bite him and chop him down with his forefeet.

Shouting his wild laughter, Miller would escape by running and vaulting over the top of the corral rails. Then he would call back to Shorty and say: "Now, dammit, Shorty, I didn't mean it. I was just playing." And Shorty would forgive him and quiet down. And Wade Miller would turn to the strangers and say, "Is it not true that the horse speaks English?"

And how could one deny it?

The Man Who Smokes Like a Chimney came to Villa Madero. He saw this demonstration and wished for the horse. But Miller had seen this one abuse horses as he did men. Miller refused; and when later he was transferred into a district where riding was unnecessary, he gave the horse to Tom Roberts, the one called *Patachica.*

Then *Patachica* went on leave to Texas. And in his absence and without his consent, The Man Who Smokes Like a Chimney came for Shorty.

He cursed the one left in charge of the horses for informing him that *Patachica* had left orders that no one was to ride his horses while he was gone. He went into the corral and roped Shorty, who was not accustomed to being roped and jerked around like a *bravo.* The Man was rough in slipping the bridle bits into Shorty's mouth and rougher in his manner of saddling, so that, when he mounted, Shorty was nervous and reared.

And that is when The Man Who Smokes Like a Chimney made his mistake. He swore the wrong gringo oath. He said, "Why, you Goddam son of a bitch!" and struck Shorty across the head with his quirt.

Which angered the frightened Shorty so that he reared higher, so high and so far that he fell to the earth backward, slamming his rider against the earth, then rolling across him.

The Man Who Smokes Like a Chimney was not killed, but it was only through God's own mercy and no fault of Shorty's. Man and horse arose from the corral dust at about the same time. With ears laid back and yellow teeth gleaming viciously, Shorty chased his rider across the corral and saw him dive to safety between the corral bars, in spite of the size of his sagging belly.

And never again would Shorty even so much as allow The Man Who Smokes Like a Chimney to enter the same corral with him, no matter whether he spoke English or Spanish.

To see a hated *matavaca* brought to justice in such a manner by a mere horse was an experience to lift one's spirit and made a tale that lost none of its savor by repeated tellings in the cantinas of Villa Madero.

A Fine Sense of Humor

Steve Lamar, post inspector at León, Guanajuato, was one gringo with a fine sense of humor that The People could appreciate.

To León came an appraiser called Jess Watson, of Laredo, Texas. He came seeking to buy cattle. These cattle, he explained to Lamar, must have received the vaccination thirty days previously. They were to be shipped to the laboratories of *La Comisión* in Mexico City, where their blood would be tested. In this manner, workers in the laboratories might determine their immunity to the sickness.

Lamar knew of such cattle and directed Watson to the ranch. He did not consider it his duty, however, to inform Watson that these cattle were the black ones, bred to fight in the bull rings of Mexico.

Watson drove to the ranch. He saw the cattle and left his truck to make a closer inspection. Barely in time did a vaquero of the ranch ride up to call out a warning.

"Have care, *señor!*" the vaquero shouted. "Already one approaches from behind."

Bill

Jess Watson glanced over his shoulder. Charging him from the rear was a black devil of a bull, his tail high, his wickedly curved horns lowered for destruction.

Ay! how that *Tejano* did run! With what great bounding leaps did he clear every rock and shrub that made an obstruction in the course he followed toward his truck. Such a speed did he develop that the tail of his shirt stood out in the breeze with a stiffness that might easily have supported the weight of a bottle of wine.

And that leap from the ground into his truck! Of a certainty, it was a distance that will not be duplicated for years.

Even so, the speed of the bull was such that at almost the very instant the *Tejano* slammed the cab door shut, the bull struck it, his horns sinking great dents into the metal and the mighty force of his charge all but overturning the vehicle.

The one called Jess Watson returned to León filled with a great desire for vengeance. But by coincidence Lamar had left town only that morning, and none of those who had laughed with him about sending the appraiser to inspect the fighting bulls knew of his destination.

Like a Black Shadow

It was said by some that trouble followed gringo Burl Duval, of Del Rio, Texas, like a black shadow.

Duval was the first to take a brigade of *La Comisión* into the vicinity of Morelia. Sent along to guard him from irate *campesinos* who resented having their cattle vaccinated were a Mexican Army sergeant, a corporal, and five privates. And among the guards was one soldier who bitterly resented all gringos.

"Mexico for the Mexicans!" this one kept saying.

When Duval failed to show resentment, the soldier climbed into the power-wagon cab with him, assumed a domineering attitude, and began giving orders.

"Drive on, my gringo chauffeur," he would command. Or, puffing his cigarette smoke into the gringo's face, he would grin and say, "How do you like that, my frightened little *matavaca?*"

When by nightfall he still had failed to arouse the hated *Tejano*, the soldier lost patience. Riding now on the back of the truck, he

-Bill-

started to shoot the white man through the cab and got knocked down by his sergeant for his trouble.

The gringo stopped his power wagon then. He got out and said to the sergeant, "Would you do me the favor of herding that one out into the road where the lights of the truck will fall upon him?"

The sergeant would. And with the first blow of a fist trained by prize-fighting in Texas, the "frightened gringo chauffeur" knocked the soldier so far out into the darkness that none could find him.

When at last they backed the truck around so that the lights might reveal the lost soldier, the other soldiers laughed aloud. Some twenty feet below the brink of a cliff that edged the road lay the brave soldier, completely unconscious.

"Let him lie there," advised a soldier. "He is a crazy one, who does nothing but smoke marijuana and seek trouble."

"No, no, no!" objected another in great concern. "He will die there, and he has money owing to me."

"But will he pay if we save him?"

"Who knows? But of a certainty, he will never pay if left there to die."

So the soldiers climbed down the rocky face of the cliff and struggled back with the limp and bleeding body of the one who smoked marijuana and borrowed money and hated all gringos. And they hauled him into town and revived him, and never again did the soldier refer to Burl Duval as his "frightened gringo chauffeur."

But that did not bring an end to Duval's trouble, because he was left with a broken fighting hand, which swelled to such alarming proportions as to resemble a cow's udder strutted with milk. For more than a week he was unable to work.

Then, just as the swelling began at last to recede, it was time for what the gringos called "a booster typhoid shot." Which was a very foolish thing indeed, since Duval allowed himself to be picked in the arm with a needle, as if he were an ox with the sickness. And no man can hope to endure as much as an ox. So, as might have been expected, his arm swelled to the size of a man's leg and the fever attacked. And on his birthday, Duval lay abed, swearing vile oaths at gringos Herb Prescott and Bill Leftwich, who, on the pretense of paying a visit to the sick, came and consumed the entire cake that Duval's wife had baked for him in honor of the occasion.

When finally recovered from the effects of the needle, Duval received orders to move to the northern part of Guanajuato to start on a second wave of livestock vaccinations. And on the way there, he drove through another village where lived another one who resented the presence of gringos in Mexico. This one hurled a rock through the open cab window. The rock struck Duval on the head, knocking him unconscious. His wife grabbed the wheel of the moving power wagon barely in time to avoid a collision with another vehicle.

But such was the nature of this gringo that when his senses returned, he shook his bloody head and smiled at his troubles.

"My luck is good," he declared. "It might have been a bullet."

Memories Are Long

In Tzintzuntzan, Michoacán, lived the owner of a cantina who was quick to welcome members of *La Comisión* when they arrived. This one had knowledge of the English and derived pleasure from demonstrating to others his familiarity with the foreign tongue. When the gringos said or did a thing beyond the comprehension of The People he could translate the words or explain the significance of the act.

This ability caused his neighbors to look up to the cantina-owner, so that he knew the sweet feeling of prominence.

The gringo called Bill Leftwich asked of him, "You have resided in the United States?"

"For nine years," said the cantina-owner. "I worked on the railroads near the great city of Chicago."

"To earn money?"

"In part, yes. But in part, it was to escape vengeance. I killed one who was my enemy and believed it best to absent myself from Mexico until his relatives had forgotten."

"And now they have forgotten?"

"Of a certainty, *señor*. For many years now, I have lived in Tzintzuntzan and known only peace."

But the relatives had not forgotten. On a day when the gringo worked with his brigade among the ranches, checking to learn of any cattle that had not been picked with the needle, two strangers rode the bus into town.

These two entered the cantina of the man who spoke the English. Each ordered a bottle of Dos Equis beer. They drank the beers and ordered two more. And when the owner of the cantina turned his back, reaching for the second drinks, they drew concealed pistols from inside their shirts and shot him in the back. Then they left the cantina and went to the station, where they boarded a returning bus.

"But did no one seek to arrest or follow the killers?" demanded Leftwich when he returned and learned of the murder.

"But no, *señor*," he was told. "That was impossible. They carried guns!"

A Matter of Politics

In Huetamo, Michoacán, politics is a science not to be taken lightly.

On this morning, Inspector Dude Warner, from Cotulla, Texas, left Huetamo, driving south with a vaccinating brigade.

In a ditch beside the road, he came upon the bodies of two dead men, each with a candle still burning beside his head.

Warner stopped his power wagon. "What is this?" he demanded of the lieutenant in command of the soldiers sent along to guard him.

The lieutenant shrugged his shoulders. "It is a matter of politics," he said.

"Politics?"

"Of a certainty, the trouble is political."

There was a finality about this political trouble that did not appeal to Dude Warner. "I think it best," he said, "that we return and work north of Huetamo today."

But beside the road that led north out of Huetamo, he came upon the bodies of two more dead men. Candles had also been placed beside the heads of these dead ones, but now the hour was late and the candles had burned out.

Warner considered for a moment, then said, "It is possible that tomorrow will be a better day for work."

The lieutenant, who was also a philosopher, nodded. "For work, *señor*, tomorrow is always a better day."

Back in town, Warner reported the murders to the *presidente municipal*, who at once commandeered Warner's power wagon to carry him out to the scenes of crime.

After a careful investigation of the first two bodies, the *presidente* said in a voice of authority: "You will note that each man has been shot between the eyes. Therefore, their deaths are not accidental."

After an equally careful investigation of the second two bodies, the *presidente* turned to Warner and asked, "*Señor*, would you do me the favor of lending me a cigarette?"

Warner had no cigarettes. His helpers had no cigarettes. Not even the soldiers had cigarettes.

So the *presidente* searched through the pockets of the dead men until he found cigarettes. But they were of the El Tigre brand, a cheap cigarette of poor quality and worse flavor. The *presidente* had taken only two puffs from one before he flung it to the ground.

"*Ay, carajo!*" he exclaimed in disgust. "What cigarettes these dead ones smoke!"

The *presidente* gave orders that burros be sent out, on which the bodies of the dead men might be loaded and transported to the cemetery. Then he hurried back to town where he could purchase cigarettes of a quality to befit one of his position.

Troops of the Mexican Twenty-seventh Infantry Battalion were called in to investigate the political murders. They arrived in a truck.

PITO
PEREZ
CALLE
JUAREZ
RIALTOS
-Bill-

Four soldiers were sent to each cantina. Two stood guard outside the cantina door, while the other two entered to ask questions and search the person of each drinker for knives and guns and other deadly weapons.

Fourteen suspects were arrested. Their hands and feet were tied. Then they were thrown into the back of the truck and hauled toward Morelia, a twenty-four-hour drive over rough roads. At Morelia, they would stand trial for their crimes.

But they never stood trial, for they never arrived at Morelia.

When the people of Huetamo learned of this, they became angry. For it is not an unheard-of thing for political prisoners to be given a chance to escape, only to be shot in the back as they run.

In secret, the angry people conferred and agreed. And they watched and waited. And one day two soldiers of the Twenty-seventh Infantry Battalion, making purchases inside a store, heard a shot and hurried out to find that their colonel had been assassinated.

The soldiers rushed about and arrested people and asked them questions and abused them with blows and curses—and learned nothing.

The colonel was assassinated? What a frightful crime! But, of course, for one who persists in playing politics, death is not an unexpected outcome.

The Canyon of Death

One who is about to travel the road between Huetamo and Santiago in southern Michoacán had best pause and consider. He should ask of himself: "Have I made an enemy of my neighbor? Have I stolen the favors of his woman? Have I butchered his pig? Have I incurred his anger over the location of a property line?"

For the road between these towns leads through a narrow pass in the mountains, where the walls of basalt stand high and sheer, and where one has little opportunity to avoid the bullet of an assassin who may lurk among the rocks.

This pass is called "The Canyon of Death," and the many crosses, sprouting like white flowers beside the road, attest to the appropriateness of the name.

The body of one who died there has been removed and buried in a cemetery, but a cross marks the spot where his spirit departed. And it is to this spot, on special days, that those who knew him come to

JUAN LOMA

pray for his soul, to place a stone beside the cross, and to place flowers upon the stones.

And the flowers may fade and wither, but the stones remain and continue to accumulate, until at last they cover the cross itself.

Even so, there may be one, possibly a secret lover, whose heart so cherishes the memory of him that in the dead of night she will brave the terrors of the death-haunted canyon to come and hold communion with him.

How else can the early-morning traveler along this road account for the presence of a rose resting in a cup atop the mound of stones, a bright red rose, with dewdrops like sparkling diamonds still clinging to its petals?

"The Canyon of Death" is a place of wild and arresting beauty. But even the fearless gringos of *La Comisión* sensed the loneliness and danger of it and were inclined to hurry through.

A Reputable Assassin

In the town of Tiquicheo, in the state of Michoacán, lived an old man and his son. Between them they owned one cow. The cow bore a calf. It was a strong, robust calf, and sight of it aroused greed in the son's heart.

The son said to his father, "This is *my* calf."

"No," the old man said. "It is but half your calf. The other half is mine."

But the son was stubborn, and they argued for days and became bitter and resentful of one another.

At last the greedy son became so angry that he hired an assassin to kill his father. The price of murder was high, two hundred pesos, but the assassin was a reputable one who could recall with justifiable pride forty assassinations performed with such remarkable skill that not once had the finger of suspicion been pointed at him or at the one who hired him.

But the greatest of skill is no wall against misfortune. In some

mysterious manner, the father learned of the plot to take his life and he made preparations for the event.

From a secret hiding place, he took a .44-caliber revolver, preserved since the days of *La Revolución*. With great care he cleaned and oiled and loaded the gun. When he slept that night, it was with the revolver lying on the floor mat beside him, the hammer drawn back to full cock.

The killer came early. In the first faint light of dawn, he knocked at the old man's door and called to him in the friendly tones of a neighbor.

He heard the old man grunt sleepily, heard the snap and crackle of his stiff old joints as he arose from his mat, heard the shuffling whisper of his bare feet on the hard-packed earthen floor as he came to the door.

Silently, the assassin drew his long murder knife and made ready to strike.

But, instead of flinging wide the door, as the killer had anticipated, the old man opened it merely a crack, saw the dark figure, saw the drawn knife, and fired.

Echoes of the shot raced through the town, shouting the alarm; but in Mexico gunfire is no uncommon thing, so The People slept on.

The old man stood, gun held ready, for the moment it took the dark figure of the assassin to sag and crumple to the ground. Then he closed the door and returned to his mat, where he resumed his sleep until the sun was warm on the side of his hut and the police came knocking at his door.

According to their duty, the police questioned the old man; but his explanation was simple and logical, and the body of the assassin, with a hole in his belly, verified his story. So the police departed to question the son. At his home they learned that only that morning the son had left early on a long journey into another state, where he had urgent business to transact.

Since, in Mexico, to chase down and apprehend a criminal who has fled to another state is seldom deemed worthy of the effort and costs involved, the police shrugged their shoulders and went back to the station.

Later in the morning, a taxi arrived from the neighboring town of Morelia. It drove up and stopped at the old man's door. The driver explained that he had been sent to pick up the body by a kinsman of the dead assassin. The kinsman was a man of some position in Morelia and could not afford to risk the possible disgrace of having it said that he would not give proper burial to a relative.

Several men of Tiquicheo who were about to make a trip to Morelia saw the taxi. They came to bargain with the driver. They argued long and heatedly and at last agreed upon the price they would pay for a ride.

The old man stood in the warm sunshine outside his house and watched the travelers depart. They rode with their feet propped up on the body of the dead assassin, while they leaned from the taxi windows and waved cheerful farewells to friends and neighbors who had come to tell them to go with God. And after they were gone, the old man spent several moments with his head bent, gravely considering a matter that had been on his mind since the day the calf was born.

At last, he came to a decision. Turning to his corral, he let down the bars and drove the cow and calf out and on across town to where members of *La Comisión* were vaccinating.

He said to the gringos: "This is *my* cow and *my* calf. It is my wish that you pick them with the needle in order that they do not take the sickness and die."

-Bill-

Peace Is a Dream

Gradually, some came to accept, others even to appreciate, the work of *La Comisión*.

Such a one was Lázaro García, *jefe* of El Rancho Canada, in the state of Michoacán, who went so far as to invite the gringos into his home.

"Come into my poor house, *señores*," he would welcome them.

And once the gringos were seated upon the boxes or upon the hard-packed earthen floor of his house, Lázaro would order his wife to bring food.

The fare was as simple as the service. To each visitor the wife brought a bowl of beans resting upon a stack of tortillas. And, to prevent possible embarrassment of any guest unaccustomed to eating without table, without knife, fork, or spoon, Lázaro would demonstrate how one removed one tortilla at a time from under the bean bowl and used it as a scoop to lift the beans to his mouth, thereby providing himself with beans and tortillas, all in one bite.

Once his guests had fed, Lázaro would then accompany them to the ranch of a neighbor and urge that one to allow his *ganado* to be picked.

The needle had merit, Lázaro assured the neighbor, not only against the *fiebre aftosa,* but against other ills of cattle and hogs.

Nonetheless, even when persuaded to co-operate, The People grew tired of *La Comisión.* They grew tired of the repeated corralling and roping and vaccinating and destroying of their livestock, of taking orders from those in command, of seeing the customs violated, of having their daughters lose their virtue to drunken *matavacas.*

So, when at last, in September of 1950, the work of *La Comisión* was said to be done, the sickness eradicated, and the workers dispersed to other parts, The People knew a profound relief.

"Now, we will have peace," they said to each other.

But hardly had *La Comisión México-Americana para la Erradicación de la Fiebre Aftosa* moved out and become *La Comisión México-Americana para la Prevención de la Fiebre Aftosa,* when those in power organized still another commission—this time for the vaccination of The People!

The People cried out in protest. "Are we cattle?" they demanded. "Are we pigs and goats and sheep, to be picked with the needle and destroyed because of our infirmities?"

"Do you prefer death from smallpox to the mere picking of a needle?" the officials demanded.

The People did, and they said so, in no uncertain tones.

But, of course, they were given no choice in the matter. In every town and village, at every crossroads and bus stop, The People were corralled by soldiers and inspected by women nurses. And unless

- Bill -

they could display upon their arms the ugly scar that proved a previous vaccination, they were forced, under threat of armed soldiers, to submit to the needle.

Apparently, for The People, the dream of peace is nothing more than a dream.